303
WRITING
PROMPTS

303 WRITING PROMPTS

Ideas to Get You Started

BONNIE NEUBAUER

FALL RIVER PRESS

New York

FALL RIVER PRESS

New York

An Imprint of Sterling Publishing
1166 Avenue of the Americas
New York, NY 10036

Book design by Kevin Ullrich
Cover design by Igor Satanovsky

ISBN 978-1-4351-6078-1

For information about custom editions, special sales, and premium
and corporate purchases, please contact Sterling Special Sales at
800-805-5489 or specialsales@sterlingpublishing.com.

Manufactured in the United States of America

2 4 6 8 10 9 7 5 3 1

www.sterlingpublishing.com

Introduction

Do any of these describe you?

❏ I want to write but haven't a clue where to begin.

❏ I used to write all the time, but lately I've been stuck.

❏ I am afraid I will write junk, so I don't write anything at all.

❏ I have a writing assignment due soon and I can't think of a topic.

❏ I write for work, but now I want to try my hand at creative writing.

❏ I know I have a book inside me, but I'm not a writer.

❏ I bought a journal and after many months, it's still empty.

❏ I teach writing and need some fresh ideas for my lesson plans.

- ❏ My writing is sporadic and I want to get into the habit of writing regularly.
- ❏ I don't have time to go to writing workshops and miss the fun exercises we did.

If so, you have come to the right place. Between these covers you will find 303 writing prompts specifically designed to help you put pen to paper or fingers to keyboard—and have fun doing it!

Imagine you are a scientist and this book is your lab. You are free to experiment with words, sentences, paragraphs, plots, characters, and genres. Some trials will be more successful than others, but it's only through doing them that you will improve and learn about your own unique writing style, voice, and practice.

To get started, open the book to a random page, read the prompt, and start writing. Don't stop and think about it, just write. It's helpful to set a time or page length goal, such as writing for only ten minutes or writing until you fill a page. While you are writing, let your mind go free. Don't try to lead

your pen or fingers; instead, let them loose on the page and watch what comes out of them. Keep your hand(s) moving forward. Don't go back and cross out; there will be plenty of time for that later.

When you are done writing, read aloud what you penned. Enjoy listening to your own creative process. When you hear something that shines, circle it. These nuggets are what you are aiming for on a regular basis.

After using writing prompts for a while, you will likely start wanting to write whatever it was that prompted you to pick up this book in the first place. So get started! Should you get stuck at any point, remember that this book is on your shelf and at the ready. Simply pick it up again, open to a random page, and it will help you get back into your flow.

I had a great time dreaming up these prompts and I hope you enjoy using them.

Write on!

1

Your story opens with two people standing on an oriental carpet.

> Where are they?
>
> Why are they there?
>
> What are they doing?
>
> Who are they?
>
> And what happens to them?

2

Write a story about a trap door that is not a mystery or a suspense story. Instead, make it a sweet, old-fashioned love story.

Also, include people with two different accents and bring it to a happy ending before you hit 400 words.

Write a cyberpunk, near-future story narrated by a half-computer, half-human who is still in school. His lessons at the moment are focused on when and how to choose emotion over logic. Every day he goes out into the world to practice what he has learned. In your story, have him make some funny errors. It's up to you whether he "gets" the humor or not.

As an extra challenge, use these words in your story: "gush," "blush," "crush."

Start with the word "dizzy" and immediately write whatever word or phrase comes to you. Let your mind free associate through stream-of-consciousness thinking as you once again write whatever comes to you based on what you just wrote. Let the words or phrases pour out of your brain onto the page, one triggering the next. Do not filter anything. Continue until you fill a whole page. If a word or phrase should prompt a story, run with it.

When the page is full, go back and read what you wrote and marvel at the way your brain works when you let it roam free. If you are ever stuck in your writing, try this to loosen things up.

5

For this piece, you will be writing about fried chicken. Anything goes here—a time you ate twenty pieces, watching someone else eat it, using a family recipe, why you hate it, what it sounds like and smells like when it is being cooked—just run with the topic.

Set a timer and write the story in six minutes. Then stop, even if you are at a sizzling, pivotal point. Leave yourself wanting more—just like the topic.

6

Write a story from the point of view of the mother of a family of immigrants who have recently arrived in America. She is a timid yet determined woman.

Start with: "Some things are like I expected, but other things..."

How many are in the family? Are there children? Where are they from? Why did they leave their country? What part of the United States are they in? Where are they staying? How do they communicate? What year is it? What do they think of America? What are their hopes and dreams about America? What do they do all day?

7

Here's how your story begins:

> *At the Bingo Hall, the moment Delia Bergonia jumped up out of her seat and shouted, "Postage stamp!" the three hall monitors, with Marie Sue Pestler in the lead, scurried toward her. Marie Sue desperately wanted to call out and confirm the numbers in Delia's winning shape. But, as had been the case for the last three episodes of "Reality Bingo," Jessie Ellen Mortisen beat her to it. This was the last time Marie Sue was going to let Jessie Ellen smile in front of the camera and flaunt her cleavage to the millions of addicted viewers; she had a plan. Marie Sue was 99.999% certain she knew how to get Jessie Ellen eliminated from the show.*

You'll have to finish the story to discover her plan and also find out if she is successful.

8

Write a story set in a steampunk world populated with fictional characters. One of these characters is you—with your full name. This means you will be referring to yourself in the third person.

Also appearing in this 500-word story will be a blimp, a chimp, and a limp.

Following the special directions below, write a four-paragraph story about two girls splashing in a pond.

> 1 — In the first paragraph, include strawberries.
>
> 2 — In the second paragraph, introduce an owl into the story.
>
> 3 — In the third paragraph, include a radio.
>
> 4 — In the fourth and last paragraph, mention a storm.

10

Write a paragraph-long description of a special hug you either gave or received.

When you are done, use this hug (or type of hug) as the turning point in a story that takes place in Poland in 1944.

Take a full page to describe the apartment (or flat) of a person who:

> Has a Type-A personality
> Collects modern-art glass sculptures
> Lives on gourmet take-out food
> Is an accountant
> Enjoys Broadway musicals

When you are done writing, answer these questions:

> What colors were prevalent?
> What textures came to the forefront?
> Was it neat or messy?
> Did it feel like a home or a museum?
> Was it peaceful or chaotic?
> What is the age and gender of the person who lives there?
> Did anything surprise you?

12

In an old black and white photograph, two boys are standing next to each other. One is pudgy, holding a ball, and wearing a cap. The other is half as tall, in diapers, and eating a cookie. They both look like they have been crying.

Place them in time, give them names and ages, and tell the story of what happened before the photo was taken.

13

Start with this famous phrase: "Slowly I turned... step by step... inch by inch..."

Then, use one of these five familiar themes to write a horror story. Use the other four themes for future writings.

> 1 — A woman alone in a dark house
>
> 2 — An experiment gone terribly awry
>
> 3 — Someone running through the forest or woods
>
> 4 — An escaped prisoner
>
> 5 — A rabid creature

14

Write a magical love story in which the image of Lincoln on a five-dollar bill winks at a woman.

15

Do a little research on a country that is currently at war or in some form of turmoil. Inspect a map to see the hot spots, read up on what the skirmishes are about, and look at the expressions on the faces of local civilians and fighters in photos.

Armed with this knowledge, imagine you are on location. You are a reporter, cowriting a photo-journalism piece with a photographer about a family that lives there.

Start your piece with this: "Imagine living at the intersection of..."

16

Write a story titled "Slow Dance" in which the characters do not dance at all. Rather, the title refers to the way in which their relationship develops and the manner in which the story is told.

17

Write a story about these four characters: Newton Tinder, Biff Malachite, Merry Masterson, Bronson Treble. All you have to go on is their names, but that should help you see the characters enough to get started.

Start with: "They didn't know it when they met…"

18

Write opening paragraphs for four different stories that each start with the same question: "Why did you do that?"

Each story must include or make reference to a ruler.

The people involved will change for each of the four story openers you write. Here are your four sets of people from which to choose:

> 1 — Teacher and student
>
> 2 — Married couple
>
> 3 — Kids at a playground
>
> 4 — Chef and sous chef

Write an exaggerated, comic-book–style superhero story.

> The hero is Superb Al, who has the ability to bounce like a superball.

> The slimy villain is Sal Amander, who can breathe both in and out of water.

> The victim in need of rescue is none other than you. Please supply your own talents as you see fit.

Does Superb Al save the day and rescue you? Do you save yourself? Or does Sal Amander convince you to come to the dark side?

20

Finish up this story by adding five more paragraphs.

It always happens like this. I lean back on the recliner, shuffle my derriere into the perfect position, adjust the headrest pillow, and fumble for the remote. Before I can even push the "on" button, my wife miraculously calls from the other room. It's inevitably some chore or another for me to do. And do immediately. There's no waiting with her. Don't get me wrong, I love her dearly. We've been married for almost sixty years. She just happens to have the worst sense of timing coupled with the best sense of recliner radar in the entire state of Florida. Nowadays, however, instead of faking a snore or grumbling, I jump up whenever she calls. You see, her memory has been slipping and we've recently had some close calls.

21

Your characters in this story are:

>   1 — A woman whose personality is
>   similar to that of a stray cat
>
>   2 — A man whose personality is more
>   like that of a house cat

Write until you finish a scene where they make up after a spat.

Start with: "We get along for long stretches and then..."

22

Write a story as told by a card player who compares the hand he was just dealt in a game with the figurative hand he has been dealt in real life.

Start with: "Usually a pair of queens isn't trouble, but..."

23

List six verbs you associate with power tools.

Now use all of them in a piece that takes place at a cocktail party. Do not mention or make reference to tools or repairs in your story.

24

Write a four-paragraph story that begins with this quote from Henry David Thoreau:

I have an immense appetite for solitude, like an infant for sleep, and if I don't get enough for this year, I shall cry all the next.

25

Write a monologue of self-talk as spoken by a person all alone, standing in front of a mirror, pumping up for and practicing a speech.

Start with: "C'mon on, now. You can do this. No one is going to..."

Write a dialogue-only conversation between two people where each line of the dialogue is no more than five words. Fill an entire page with it.

Time to practice writing some description. Fill an entire page with the description of a single house—exterior only—from the list of ten below. Return again to try your hand at the other nine.

1 — Victorian mansion

2 — Beach bungalow

3 — Swiss chalet

4 — Converted barn

5 — Thatched-roof cottage

6 — Hunting lodge

7 — Tree house

8 — Wooden shack

9 — Houseboat

10 — Log cabin

28

I nvent a story about people who have a secret plan to meet at midnight under the twelfth tree in the twelfth row of an apple orchard.

29

Think about three different times in your life where eggs played a major role. Write three separate paragraphs, one about each.

Examples: dying Easter eggs, making a special omelet, learning about eggs and the reproductive system, dropping a carton of eggs on the floor.

After you have completed your three paragraphs, turn them into an essay by adding an introduction, transitional sentences, and a conclusion. Title it "My Life, Eggsactly."

30

Start with this:

> *Garth stared out the frosty, grimy windows of the cabin as he watched the violent snow spin across his family's fields. The wind gusts had damaged the gate he and his dad had built back in the summer and the animals were now in danger. With the toe of his boot, he anxiously dug a hole in the dirt floor. He was under strict orders to stay in the house with his baby sister until his parents returned home...*

Finish the story.

31

In a parking lot you found a slip of paper with the following to-do list on it:

> CB Gram, Ed
>
> Suit—Cleaner
>
> Buy TP, PT
>
> Bank Dep
>
> Wine
>
> Shoes for Wed
>
> Res. Hotel
>
> Car Oil
>
> DON'T FORGET—TXT Melody Re SAT!

Based solely on this list, describe in detail the person who lost it, the crisis he or she is currently embroiled in, and how he or she is going to fix it.

32

Write a story that includes these three made-up words: "EVARGAE," "SNIREK," "MOSNAR." They can be anything you like: names, places, adjectives, verbs. Let your instincts choose, and let your reader deduce the meaning through context.

Start with this phrase: "The payoff seemed worth the risk..."

Write a story that uses these sensory combinations: the sound of clouds, the taste of a book, the feel of an echo.

Start with: "When I lifted my arm..."

34

Think of peeling and eating a delicious, juicy orange. Jot down some of the smells, textures, and flavors that come to mind. Use all the phrases and words you wrote down in a story that has absolutely nothing to do with oranges.

Start your story with this: "The computer kept spitting out data that made no sense. It was as if..."

35

If you are ever in need of a quick writing exercise, simply start with the word "I," add a verb, then fill a page. Here are twenty-six, one for each letter of the alphabet, to get you started:

> I asked, I begged, I called, I didn't,
> I expected, I found, I gave, I helped,
> I imitated, I joked, I kicked, I laughed,
> I met, I noticed, I opened, I prayed,
> I questioned, I raced, I stole, I took,
> I understood, I voted, I wished,
> I (e)xamined, I yearned, I zipped.

Pick one now and fill an entire page. I invite you to come back and use the other twenty-five.

36

Take a moment to touch one (or both) of your cheeks. Think about the many kisses that have been planted there. Tell the story of one of those kisses.

37

Use one of your recurring dreams to fuel this story. Instead of waking up in the middle of the dream, play it out. See what happens; let your pen lead the way. If you don't happen to have a recurring dream, use this one: You are walking to school, unprepared for a test, and you don't have any pants on.

To get you started, begin with this phrase: "It's always the same..."

38

Here is your opening:

All told, jail isn't as bad as I expected. I haven't seen any fights, nor have I heard any of that nonstop screaming they always show in the movies. Don't get me wrong, it's pretty awful in here and I'd rather be out. But I can handle it. What I can't take is that my wife doesn't believe me. I have told her a dozen times now that I am not guilty. Whenever I put in a collect call to her, she is polite to the operator who connects us. And then when we are alone on the line, she screams at me and shouts accusations. I have pleaded with her to listen to me, but she always breaks down into loud sobs.

Finish the story.

39

Write a historical story that takes place during the time of the suffragettes (female activist supporters of women's right to vote in the late nineteenth and early twentieth centuries).

Do a little research on suffragettes so that you will be able to include vivid and realistic details.

Write from the point of view of a suffragette's spouse. Does he agree with his wife's cause? What does he do when she goes to jail for it?

40

Write a story about sibling rivalry where the main character is an antihero. Antiheroes are unconventional central characters who lack the virtues of traditional heroes, but readers still feel sympathy for them. Often they are dreamers, misfits, comics, or even downright louses. Sometimes they are the people you love to hate. Make your antihero witty and charming with some emotional depth so that your readers have some emotional investment in him or her.

Start with: "He/She was almost…"

Write an entire story as a series of journal or diary entries written by one person. Reveal deep emotions, unspoken secrets, and intimate details. Also make sure to spread a good dose of humor or irony through the entries. This can be achieved through repetition of unmet goals, self-deprecating humor, or some other technique. The number of entries and time span between them is for you to decide.

42

Outline a story that will take place during one day. Chronicle each event that happens in half-hour increments from morning to night.

Once you have an outline, try writing the story in less than a day.

43

Write a story that includes these three items:

    1 — An actor

    2 — An engine

    3 — A tangerine

Start the story with this phrase: "Under the…"

44

You are the middle C key of a piano. Write from the key's point of view.

Start with: "Whenever she sits down on the bench, I..."

Start with:

> *Miles hesitantly, and a bit awkwardly, reached across the table for Marjorie's hand. He had momentarily held it at the end of their last date when he had chickened out of leaning in for a kiss. A week and a day later, its silkiness still echoed in his palm. In time, Miles knew he would also touch Marjorie's other hand, the one with the prosthetic. But right now he focused all his energy on her right hand, hoping she would place it in his.*

Finish the story.

46

To get into character for this exercise, you first need to change how old you are. Take the two numbers for your age and reverse them. If you are twenty-nine, for this exercise you are now ninety-two. If your age is two digits of the same number, remove one of the digits. This would turn you from a thirty-three-year old to a three-year old. If you are a single-digit age, double the digit. As an example, you would go from being nine to being ninety-nine.

One change isn't enough, however. You must also change to the opposite sex.

With these two changes in place, write, starting with: "Of all the places in the world, I never expected to..."

47

Sometimes talking to people who you are certain you will only meet once is very freeing. In this writing, you are visiting a town for one day. While getting your hair cut, tell the hair dresser about your mother.

Start with: "Getting my hair cut reminds me of..."

According to Ernest Hemingway, "Break off work when you 'are going.' Then you can rest easily and on the next day easily resume."

Today write with the starter provided. However, just when you are really getting into it, STOP. Put away your pen and get on with the rest of your day. Come back the next day and pick up where you left off.

Your starter is: "He stopped at..."

Is Hemingway right? Did this work for you?

Write a story whose title is "Double Trouble." In it, two symbols play a pivotal role.

Choose your symbols from this list:

> crucifix
>
> swastika
>
> Gordian knot
>
> ankh
>
> Iron Cross
>
> fish
>
> Hand of Fatima
>
> mandala
>
> pentagram
>
> yin-yang
>
> totem
>
> crescent moon
>
> fleur-de-lys
>
> dream catcher

50

Finish this story:

> *I am sure they do it partly to intimidate us, and partly out of lack of any other available seating arrangement. Whatever the case, sitting on that small chair at my kid's desk with my legs up to my nostrils was way unpleasant. You'd think teachers would have figured out by now that a comfortable parent is a more compliant parent. But there I was, waiting for Mr. Plymth so I could plead my case about Jake for the third time since September. This time I promised myself to not lie and say what a great kid he is at home.*

For the teacher's voice, use lots of words that include hard-sounding letters like "k" and "g."

Write an article for a local print or online news-paper about a person named Robert "R.C." Collins who is retiring after fifty years of working on the railroad. Bring him and his accomplishments to life.

Start with: "When Robert 'R.C.' Collins first..."

Write a story with a character who has these physical traits: tall, lanky, acne scars, freckles, ginger hair, crooked front teeth, start of a beard.

Start with: "His boots..."

When you are done, add one new trait to the above list of character descriptions—tattoos covering both arms. Write about this new character, also starting with: "His boots..."

53

Write a fantasy story that includes a storm, a warlock, and a compromise. Personify the storm so that it has human traits, including speech.

54

Try your pen at a story about a person whose job is to polish all the stars on the Hollywood Walk of Fame. In it, include a surprising encounter with a celebrity he or she admires as well an incident with a tourist who starts off mean and then changes his tune.

Create an over-the-top romance story by using as many of these phrases as you can:

"Seductively, his gaze slid downward..."
"She tore herself away with an audible gasp..."
"His mere presence made her insides tingle..."
"She blushed a vivid scarlet..."
"Her eyes widened in astonishment..."
"The anticipation was palpable..."
"He flashed a grin in her direction..."
"She surrendered completely..."
"He cupped her chin in his large hand..."
"Her fingers dug into his flesh..."
"He unbuttoned her blouse with confident hands..."
"Her ivory skin called out to him..."
"Her lips burned..."
"His urgent kiss said it all..."

Artists take paper and pencil out into the world and sketch what's around them. Your assignment today is to take paper and pen with you to either a park, a mall, a bus station, or a busy city street corner.

Record (sketch) smells, sounds, actions around you, tidbits of conversations, building descriptions, or items from nature.

When you get home, write a story—with a strong emphasis on location—that takes place there.

57

Start with:

> It was 7:30 a.m. when she pulled open the curtains of her penthouse hotel room. There before her, sharing the morning sky, were both a huge moon and the bright sun. The sight took her breath away and she...

Finish the story.

58

Write a story about an art heist. At the start, all your characters are hiding inside ductwork and have to whisper back and forth.

Start with: "Didja hear that?..."

59

Talk Like Shakespeare Day is April 23. Why wait until then? Write as if you live in the time of Shakespeare right now.

Here are some suggestions to make your writing sound like it is from the era:

> Use "ye," "thou," and "thee."
>
> Insert a rhymed couplet for good measure.
>
> Refer to your friends as "Cousins."
>
> Add in a few "methinks," "mayhaps," and "wherefores."
>
> Don't forget to include "'tis" and "t'will."
>
> And of course, you can always add "eth" to the end of any verb, like "runneth" and "falleth."

Start with: "Wooing ladies isn't near as simple as..."

Start with:

> *Me and Ma and Alby, we used to do what you call Dumpster divin', just about every night. It was how we got us most of our food. We was dirt poor after Ma caught Pa stealin' and booted him. It was just the three of us then, but Alby was too young to remember any of this. Anyways, every night while we was waitin' for the manager of the food store to lock up, Ma would always say, "Remember— pickin' trash ain't stealin'. I ain't raisin' no thieves." After the manager walked past us—we was hidin' in the bushes by the bank—Ma had us count real quiet up to 500 before we...*

Finish the story.

61

Start a story with:

> *We interrupt this broadcast to bring you a special emergency announcement. Repeat. This is an emergency announcement. The White House just confirmed that today, at approximately 5:15 p.m. Eastern Time, off the shore of Miami Beach, Florida...*

Take it from here.

Fill in the blanks in the sentence below and then finish the story:

The first time I heard _____[song title] _____ *I was* _____[place]_____. *I immediately...*

∞∞∞∞

Complete this story:

> *Every evening, in his thick Russian accent,*
> *he read Chekov to...*

Cross-County RV Trip Blog

Welcome. Please stop back often to read about all our RVing adventures.

Day #1

It's only our first day, but we already had quite an adventure. Suffice it to say that we are definitely learning the lessons of the road. This is how it went today:

"Honey, did you see the sign that there's a 14-foot covered bridge up ahead?"

"I see the bridge. It's over there. How romantic!"

"Um, do you remember what the rental place said was the max height for this thing?"

"Definitely in the teens. Paperwork's in the kitchen drawer. I'll check."

"Hurry. There's no place to pull over."

"I'm on it!"

"Crap!"

Finish the blog post.

The film *Back to the Future* closes with these words:

"Roads? Where we're going we don't need roads."

Use them as the first two sentences in a new story that is not at all related to the theme or plot of that movie.

66

Starting lines come in all lengths. Choose one that appeals to you and write until you fill a whole page.

> *Restlessly...*
>
> *Eleanor hoped...*
>
> *Our forefathers didn't...*
>
> *The warm, aromatic smells...*
>
> *Wishing might not work, but...*
>
> *Martians are more friendly than...*
>
> *Hidden between two pages of my...*
>
> *In the depths of the ocean lurked two...*

Remember to return to this page seven more times and try the others, too.

67

Compose four unique, very short memoir pieces. In each one, you will create and use a simile that involves a food.

Note: a simile is a figure of speech in which two unlike things are compared. The things are usually connected with the words "like" or "as." "As American as apple pie" or "She sings like an angel" are common similes.

For this exercise, if your word were "ketchup," you might create a simile like one of these: "I was so sick I moved like ketchup stuck in the bottle," or "From the very start, we complemented each other like ketchup on a hamburger."

The foods to turn into similes for your four short memoir pieces are: maple syrup, mints, mustard, margarine.

68

Using denim as a starting point, go through your life, year by year, and recall episodes and memories that are triggered by this fabric. When you find a juicy memory, run with it and write the story.

69

Write a story that includes the following five words. Each has more than one meaning, so feel free to choose whichever definition best suits your story:

1 — solution

2 — season

3 — hatch

4 — hamper

5 — harbor

Start with: "Misery loves company..."

70

Write a story in which a character is carrying a backpack. It has six items in it. Each of those items plays a crucial role in the story. At the end of the story, the backpack will be empty. What are the items? What happens?

71

Using the suggestions below, write a complete story in three paragraphs. Your main character is the opposite sex from you, but exactly your age.

> 1 — In the first paragraph, your character is torn between two things.

> 2 — In the middle paragraph, your character makes a confession.

> 3 — In the final paragraph, your character moves on.

For this prompt, you will need to do a tiny bit of research. Pick a topic from the seven listed below about which you know very little. Look it up, and then use what you learn to fortify your writing. Come back and try this again with the other topics that are not familiar to you.

1 — How to build a yurt

2 — How and why a cat purrs

3 — How forks came to be

4 — Why buttons are on opposite sides of clothing for males and females

5 — How a cable bridge works

6 — The origin of the barbershop pole

7 — How to determine the different carats of gold

Start with: "I am not the kind of person who..."

You take an old book off the shelf in a used bookstore. When you open it, something falls out.

What is it? What do you do with it? Who do you show it to? How does it change your day?

74

You are on an airplane that is starting to taxi for takeoff. You look out the window and see something or someone that causes you to call out, "Stop the plane!"

What did you see? What happens?

75

Here are five traits to help you create a character:

  1 — hardworking

  2 — protective

  3 — forgetful

  4 — blue-eyed

  5 — rough around the edges

Continue adding traits until you can see a person emerge. Once you have a visual, write from this character's point of view.

Start with: "When the bell rang..."

76

Write a story with the following components:

Who — a hip-hop star

What — a wrench

When — August 2002

Where — Baltimore

It's up to you to supply the why as you write, starting with: "It was so hot..."

Start with:

> *There's nothing quite like the sound of vinyl spinning on a turntable. If you listen closely, like putting your ear to a shell, you can hear not only the album's music, but also the history of the modern world— with all its scratches and successes. The other day when I played...*

Finish the story.

Lewis Carroll firmly believed this tenet: "What is the use of a book without pictures or conversations?"

To honor him, try this: Find a magazine and open to a random page. If there is a picture on it, you are good to go. If not, open again until you find one.

Using this picture as a jumping-off point, and including some dialogue, start the story with: "He looked up and asked, 'Why do...'"

Pick a year from your past that you particularly enjoyed. Google it and find five interesting things that happened that year, such as inventions, deaths, births, elections, or special events. Write them down.

Use this year and these tidbits from it as a backdrop to a piece that begins with: "I picked..."

80

Try writing a how-to piece composed completely of numbered bullet points.

Here's your topic: How to Start Procrastinating.

81

W rite a piece titled "How To Miss The Bus."
Base it on personal experience.

82

Think about a time when you were treated badly by someone who was supposed to be your friend. Write to this person now and tell him or her how you felt back then. Let out all the emotion on the page now.

Try this: Imagine walking out the front door of your home. As soon as you have the opportunity to do so, turn left. Walk until you can turn right. Continue walking until you pass four opportunities to turn left. At the fifth, make the turn and then stop.

Now start writing as you answer these questions:

Where are you?

What do you see?

Are you alone?

Is there a surprise waiting for you here?

What do you do while in this space?

Start with: "When I turned…"

84

Take a mental trip back in time to the home of a relative. Make it a place you haven't visited in at least ten years. As you mentally walk toward and through the home, write about the street, the landscape, the door, the entryway, the rooms, etc. Do your best to evoke the textures, smells, and sounds that are in the home, too.

After your written tour, return to a room where you had a long-ago memorable experience. Write that story now.

Start with: "I remember when..."

85

For this exercise, you will be writing about an actual promise you made but did not keep. Rather than write in the first person, use the third person: "she" or "he." Feel free to give your character a name other than your own if that helps you gain some distance from the broken promise. Embellish to your heart's content, or keep it completely true.

Start with: "When I said..."

Copy this sentence onto the middle of your page: "Amidst all the chaos, she managed to find some order."

Start writing from the top of the page until you get to this sentence—and then continue writing after it—until you finish the story.

You have the blues. Nothing sounds fun. Everything is an effort. Nothing is at all interesting. You keep comparing yourself to others who seem happy and successful. If you had one, you'd throw a rock at all the vacation photos posted by happy people on Facebook. All you want to do is have a big pity party.

Party? Did someone say party?

Describe a pity party that you might throw for yourself. Include location, libations, food, music, decorations, and maybe even a guest list. Or do you prefer to party alone?

88

Write a list titled "Ten Things I Don't Like to Think About."

Pick one of the ten items and write about it until you fill an entire page.

Think about an election that was important to you. Also think about the birth of someone special to you. Now write a story where they are both taking place at the exact same time. Write about how you participate in both and the difficult choices and decisions you make.

Start with: "I was part of..."

90

Write the story of a closet in which you played or hid.

Start with: "It was darker than I expected..."

91

In our lives we search for many things—happiness, jobs, friends, love, relatives, ancestors, our roots, our keys, answers, a mate, the remote control, words, and peace, to name some. Pick one from this list and write about a time when you looked in all the wrong places.

Start with: "They always say it's in the last place you look..."

Over the years, our bodies amass many stories. Sometimes we have visual proof of these stories in the form of scars. Other times, if we touch one of our kneecaps or toes in just the right way, stories return to us.

Take a minute or so to touch the area around one of your eyes. Feel your eyebrow hairs, the soft skin below them, perhaps crow's feet on the side. Let memories return to you. Remember things like falling off your bike and getting a cut above your eyelid, or the first time you plucked your eyebrows, or how your long eyelashes have received compliments. Tell one of these stories now. If nothing comes, feel free to make something up.

Is there something you enjoy doing and at which you are somewhat an expert? Baking strawberry-rhubarb pie, collecting fossils, drawing animé, playing guitar, doing Sudoku, shooting hoops, or something else?

Write about the person who taught you how to do this and what it was like to learn from them.

Start with: "Patience..."

94

Choose an event from your life when you felt extremely alive. Describe where you were, what you were doing, with whom, why, and how you felt—physically and emotionally—before, during, and after.

Start with:

> *Our search and rescue team gathered in front of the school, now deemed ground zero for the effort. Strategy was discussed and jobs were divvied up. Bill and I were assigned to head southwest about three-tenths of a mile before starting our search efforts. The terrain was...*

Finish the story.

96

The film *Stand By Me* ends with these words:

> *I never had any friends later on like the ones I had when I was twelve. Jesus, does anyone?*

Use that sentiment as the basis for a new story that is not at all related to the theme or plot of that film.

Starting lines come in all lengths. Choose one of these eight that appeals to you and write until you fill a whole page.

1 — Normally...

2 — After midnight...

3 — The wealthy stranger...

4 — His mama spoiled him...

5 — Worry was her middle name...

6 — The loud, pounding sound of the...

7 — Should this fail, wait three days and...

8 — Everyone referred to her as the Cat Lady...

Remember to return to this page seven more times and try the others, too.

98

Write a poem (or a rap) about not wanting to write a poem (or a rap). Write the entire thing using rhymed couplets.

While cleaning out the attic of a large home that you just bought, you come upon an old camera. You hold it up, look through the lens, and make believe you are taking a photo. When you hit the button, however, it sounds like a real photo was taken. You shoot a few more just to be sure and then open the camera. You remove the film and immediately take it to a local photo shop to be developed.

After about thirty-five minutes, you get a call from the kid who does the developing, begging you to return to the store. All he will tell you is that the photos are very disturbing.

Write the story from here.

100

The teacher is calling roll. She calls out, "Wilhelm, Marcus." You slide back your heavy wooden chair, rise from behind your desk, and politely answer, "Present."

Before sitting back down, you notice that you are in brown knickers with buttoned boots on your feet. The floor is packed dirt. You sense that physically you are a thirteen-year-old boy from another place and time. But intellectually and emotionally, you know you are still the you of today.

Time travel? A dream? Something else? Tell the story of what happens.

Start with: "Instead of sitting back down, I was frozen in place, trying to…"

Compose a story about someone who leaves behind a ten-word note. Include the text of the entire note within the body of the story.

Start your story with this phrase: "Like musical notes..."

You are a singer-songwriter, working on a new song titled "Caught Between Think and Do." The chorus is done:

> *I can't get a move-on;*
> *I'm treading in thick goo;*
> *I am stuck, yeah, I'm stuck;*
> *Caught between think and do.*

Now you need some verses. Brainstorm three times in your life when you didn't know how to take the first step, or were too frozen to move on.

Describe each of these in paragraph form and then turn all three into verses for the song.

Who knows. Maybe it will be a crossover hit!

103

Here is how your story should start:

> *The cards were dealt, the bets were placed, the stakes were high. The cameras were running.*

Describe what happens next.

104

Here are five traits to help you create a character:

1 — messy

2 — nervous

3 — soft hands

4 — hat-wearing

5 — creative

Continue adding traits until you can see a person emerge. Once you have a visual, write from this character's point of view.

Start with: "We exchanged glances…"

105

Write a story with the following components:

     Who — a cab driver

     What — a cigar

     When — 1938

     Where — a city street

It's up to you to supply the why as you write, starting
with: "I pulled over..."

Start with:

> *Billy used to think that mushroom clouds were something writers made up to ensure that movie plots would be extra-terrifying or comic book stories super-scary. Sadly, he now knows the truth; he is living in the aftermath of one such cloud. He hates wearing his gas mask, but the thing that troubles him most is that he will never...*

Finish the story.

Think of a time when you were pushed to your limits. Write down a handful of words or phrases to describe how you felt. Use all the phrases and words in a story.

Start your story with this: "The nonstop beeping of my phone..."

108

Start with:

> *They had wanted a boy.*

Finish the story.

American soldiers in World War II had their own lingo. You are now one of these soldiers, hanging out at the barracks, trading stories. Here are some words and phrases to use:

> Army strawberries—prunes
> Beat your gums—talk a lot about a topic
> Behavior report—letter to a girl
> Blow it out your barracks bag—shut up,
>   or go to hell
> Browned off—fed up
> Devil's piano—machine gun
> DoDo—air force cadet before he starts flying
> Eggs—bombs
> French leave—AWOL
> Kite—airplane
> Mae West—either an inflatable rubber
>   lifebelt, or a tank with two protuberant
>   turrets
> Maggie's drawers—red flag on a rifle range
>   to indicate a miss
> Sugar report—letter from a sweetheart

Start with: "It was about three in the morning when..."

110

Six-word memoirs are all the rage. What about a six-paragraph memoir?

Write about a time in your life when you had to make a choice between two things or were forced to make an important decision.

Keep the story to six short paragraphs and do your best to link your ending back to your beginning.

Start with: "The more I wavered..."

111

The Scoville Scale, named in 1912 for its creator, Wilbur Scoville, an American pharmacist, is the measurement of the heat of peppers and other spicy food. For example, a bell pepper is a 0, a banana pepper is 100, a jalapeno starts at 1,000, regular Tabasco sauce hits around 2,500, and a chipotle pepper falls in the 3,500 range. Habaneros or Scotch bonnets are somewhere in the 100,000 to 350,000 range and Carolina reapers top the scale at 2,200,000.

You are a pompous young guy who believes you have the capacity to handle anything and everything on the Scoville Scale. And so you are put to the test.

Start with: "We gave the cocky kid a loaf of white bread, a glass of milk, a pitcher of water, started him off with Grandma's mild chili, and then..."

Compose a story about a nurse who has been asked to perform a task that compromises his or her ethics. Use interior dialogue/monologue to show the nurse's thoughts, feelings, and fears.

For this exercise, read the following paragraph and then continue the story by writing another couple paragraphs.

Read the beginning of Edward Salisbury Field's 1909 novel, *Cupid's Understudy*:

> *If Dad had been a coal baron, like Mr. Tudor Carstairs, or a stock-watering captain of industry, like Mrs. Sanderson-Spear's husband, or descended from a long line of whisky distillers, like Mrs. Carmichael Porter, why, then his little Elizabeth would have been allowed to sit in the seat of the scornful with the rest of the Four Hundred, and this story would never have been written. But Dad wasn't any of these things; he was just an old love who had made seven million dollars by the luckiest fluke in the world.*

Now continue the story without reading anything else from Field.

A guide dog named Tarot was recently assigned to a twenty-five-year-old veteran who was blinded a year ago in a military accident. Your story takes place the first time Tarot is alone with his new owner, Leap, who is angry he has to have a guide dog.

Write the story from the point of view of Tarot.

When you are done, write the exact same story as told by Leap.

In pencil, draw a big outline of a basic fish shape on a sheet of paper. The image should cover as much of the page as possible. In ink, write inside—and only inside—the fish until you fill up all the white space. The main focus of the piece needn't be a fish, but make sure to at least reference one in your writing. When you are done writing, go back and erase the penciled fish. When you hold up the page, the fish shape will really stand out.

Start with: "I caught a cold..."

116

Write a story that includes these three items:

     1 — A party

     2 — A quiz

     3 — A rat

Start the story with this phrase: "As soon as we were…"

117

Compose one long opening paragraph whose goal is to establish atmosphere/mood/tone for a story about claustrophobia. Use location, weather, colors, sounds, and other sensory stimuli to accomplish your mission.

Write an espionage story that ends in a
suspenseful cliff-hanger. Include at least
one aspect of physical danger, a narrow escape,
and a U.S. president in your story.

Here are six names and six occupations. Pair up a name and a job and then write from this person's point of view. If you enjoy this, there are many more combos left for you to use.

1 — Sheila DiDillo

2 — Leroy Durango

3 — Murray Schwartz

4 — Lily Parsnip

5 — Kusha Patel

6 — Sai Cheng

1 — French teacher

2 — Sheriff

3 — Minister

4 — Trumpet player

5 — CEO, pharmaceutical co.

6 — Realtor

Start with: "When push comes to shove..."

Fill in the blanks in the sentence below and then finish the story:

The first time I visited [place or person], I was [describe an emotion] because no one had told me..."

Think about all the shoes you own. Pick a pair and write about something that happened to you while wearing them.

122

Write a story about six coworkers forced to carpool due to a transit strike. The entire story should take place in a car. Use all dialogue and no narrative.

Start with: "Don't you think it would be better if..."

Think of a time when finances were tight and you didn't have enough money. Jot down some of the words and phrases that you uttered during this time or use now to describe this period.

Use as many of these as you can in a story. Start your story with this: "The box of chocolates was…"

Fill in these sentences based on a character named Alana Jo Sheffert:

Once a month, she _____

At least ten times a day, she _____

Whenever she feels frustrated,
she _____

She collects _____

She loves to _____

She should really stop _____

When her alarm clock goes off,
she _____

Now write about her starting with this phrase: "It isn't easy being..."

Talk Like a Pirate Day is fun. But when you're a writer, you can write like a pirate any day of the year. Here are some pirate-y expressions (other than "ahoy," "matey," "yo-ho-ho," "aye," and "shiver me timbers") to help you along.

> Avast—a command to stop or desist
> Blimey!—an exclamation of surprise
> Dredgie—ghost of a pirate dead by
>   betrayal
> Hearties—term used to refer to fellowship
>   among sailors
> Hornswaggle—to cheat or trick
> Kiss the gunner's daughter—A punishment
>   consisting of being hoisted over one of
>   the ship's guns and flogged
> No prey, no pay—A common pirate law
>   meaning a crew received no wages,
>   but rather shared whatever loot was
>   taken
> Swag—loot

Start with: "Everybody says that dead men tell no tales. But I know otherwise, so ye best listen up. We had just battened down the hatches..."

126

When writing about people, age is something you can show rather than tell.

In a full sentence, describe each of these as if for a ninety-year-old woman.

> Her hands...
>
> Her reflexes...
>
> Her skin...
>
> Her voice...

Now do the same for a seventeen-year-old girl.

> Her hands...
>
> Her reflexes...
>
> Her skin...
>
> Her voice...

Notice the differences and use them in your writing.

Start with:

> We spent the summer on the outskirts of a tiny village along the coast of Italia. We were not typical tourists who felt compelled to visit a museo every day or go to the five-star ristorante listed in the guida turistica. We slipped right into the lifestyle of the locals. Every morning we would have our caffè on the little porch of our villa. And then we would stroll into town, waving to our neighbors, calling out, "Buon giorno" and "Come sta?" and "Ciao." But one morning, no one returned our greetings. Everyone turned their backs when we passed. We were confused, not to mention insulted. What had changed? We found out as soon as we got into town, where the polizia were waiting for us.

Finish the story.

A lthough most how-to pieces contain bulleted lists, they don't have to. Write a how-to article that is completely in paragraph form.

Your topic: How to Ignore Exercise Equipment.

Do you have any unfinished pieces of writing lying around? If so, go grab one. Don't read through it. Rather, open to the last page and scroll all the way to the bottom. Copy the last sentence on the page onto a clean sheet of paper. Use this sentence as your starter and write. Don't worry about continuity with what had been written in the other piece. The goal here is to get your pen moving again with this piece of writing.

When you are done writing, decide if what you just wrote helped to reignite interest in this piece. If it did, go back to page one and read the original from the start. While reading, as soon as you feel the urge to start writing, put a big star on the original document to mark where you left off. Put the same star at the top of a new page and begin your writing.

130

In your mind, visit the first school you attended. Start writing as soon as the school starts to come into vision. Write an entire and detailed walk-through, describing the grounds, the entrance, the halls, the stairs, the offices, the classes, etc. Try to capture the textures, smells, and sounds, too.

After completing your written tour, go back to a location in the school that holds a powerful memory. Write about it now, starting with: "I am in…"

131

In this story, you are visiting a town for one day. You will never see any of the people in the cafe ever again. Tell the barista how you were homeless up until a year ago.

Start with: "One freezing cold day, a kind woman..."

Start a story with:

> Hanging on the wall of the Astral Perfection Bistro's bathroom was a set of instructions for astral projection. If the date had not been going fairly well so far, I'd have immediately given them a try. I am a journalist, and it's in my blood to disprove hokey theories. But instead of following the directions, which included things like soaping up dry hands and crouching in front of a sink, I went back to the table. I started yawning, laying the ground work for ending the date early. My plan succeeded, and I was back in the bistro bathroom in less than half an hour. Perhaps one reason I am not married is that I much prefer debunking to bunking-up.

Continue the story.

133

Compose a story in which the main character wakes up to find that she or he is the last person on earth.

Then the phone rings...

134

Write a magazine-length feature profile piece about a person who is extremely frugal. Do not merely tell your reader this; rather, show it. You can accomplish in part by lavishly describing dramatic examples of the character's behavior, like starring on an extreme couponing television show or camping out thirteen nights to be first in line for a free gift or winning a home makeover for recycling the most items in the entire community.

For your article, also write a sidebar of tips for your readers.

Here are five traits to help you create a new location for a story:

    1 — suburban

    2 — under renovation

    3 — busy

    4 — decorated

    5 — upscale

Continue to add descriptive words until you can actually see the location. When you have a visual, write a story that takes place in this place.

Start with: "Everyone assembled..."

For this exercise, find a book with chapters in a genre you don't normally read—or write.

Open the book to a random page, let your finger drop onto it, and write down the word on which it lands. If it's a short word like "the" or "a," try again. Do this until you have four words on your page.

Now flip through the book until you come to the first page of a chapter. Copy the opening sentence onto your page. Use this sentence as your starter and include all four words in this piece. Make sure you write in the same new-to-you genre as the book you chose.

137

Make up a story where your main character is the victim of identity theft. Have him or her use words that help the reader hear the anger. Words with sibilant consonant sounds—"s," "sh," "ch," "j"— should work well because they are intense and get the reader to pay attention. Here are some examples of words with these sibilants to get you started: "shoot," "choke," "sneak," "jerk."

Start with

> *Lottie was sure of one thing—the gar-*
> *ish wallpaper from the 1970s had to be*
> *stripped from the walls before they moved*
> *in. Armed with all the necessary tools and*
> *dozens of snacks, she and Roger commit-*
> *ted an entire weekend to the task. They*
> *decided to start in what had originally been*
> *the parlor room of the old Victorian house.*
> *They were thrilled when the paper came*
> *off easily. But unfortunately, it revealed*
> *yet another layer of wallpaper beneath it.*
> *Below that was still another, much, much*
> *older layer. When they finally got to the*
> *actual wall, they discovered over 100 hash*
> *marks drawn on it as well as a bunch of*
> *arrows leading into the closet along an*
> *outside wall...*

Finish the story.

303 WRITING PROMPTS

139

Write a thank-you note or email to someone who recently said or did something that brought a smile to your face. Remind that person of what he or she did to make you smile. Tell the person how it made you feel. And when you're done, send the letter. More than likely, your letter will trigger a smile on that person's face, too.

140

If you are ever in need of a quick writing exercise, simply start with the word "she," add a verb, then fill a page. Here are twenty-six, one for each letter of the alphabet, to get you started:

> She answered, She believed, She carried, She dove, She experimented, She forgot, She grieved, She hoped, She initiated, She jammed, She knew, She learned, She made, She negated, She operated, She picked, She queried, She raged, She spoke, She tormented, She uttered, She vowed, She wrote, She (e)xpected, She yelled, She zoned out.

Pick one now and fill an entire page. I invite you to come back and use the other twenty-five.

141

Sentence starters that are not stated in a positive manner make your brain dig underneath the obvious and come up with deeper writing topic ideas. When you start with "I don't remember," your brain first filters through the things you do recall and then searches below the obvious for a topic with more depth.

Pick one of these ten negative approaches and run with it. Remember to come back and try the other nine.

1 — I don't hear...

2 — I couldn't imagine...

3 — I wasn't included...

4 — I didn't prepare...

5 — I wasn't chosen...

6 — I hadn't thought...

7 — I wasn't asked...

8 — I didn't grasp...

9 — I didn't follow...

10 — I wasn't ever...

Start with:

> *Many decades ago, Irv Chuvosky hid a small hand-mirror behind a Victrola phonograph in the back of his antique store. Both had been gifted to him by his great-aunt, Sasha Ester, who made him swear he would never sell either. After Irv died, the business passed through several hands over a couple generations. None of his ancestors ever bothered to move or sell the Victrola because it just seemed to belong in that back corner. Besides, none had ever really shown much passion for antiques; it was simply the family business. But today, as part of the going-out-of-business sale, the Victrola was moved. And the gold mirror, covered in cobwebs, was unearthed.*

Finish the story.

143

Pick one of these starters and write your heart out. If you still have emotional energy left, do another one. If not, return another time.

      1 — Racism shouldn't...

      2 — Sexism won't...

      3 — Ageism can't...

144

You are a precocious three-year-old who is quite articulate about your needs and preferences. Write a toddler diatribe about toilet training.

Start with: "If I had my way..."

The content you choose to include in a story as well as the manner in which you relay it are directly related to your audience. To experience these differences, write as if you are a fifty-five-year-old woman who was mugged.

Tell the story of your mugging to each of these four people:

        1 — Your best friend

        2 — Your child

        3 — A police officer

        4 — Your therapist or doctor

Start with:

> *I'm a counter. Yup, that's right: a counter.
> I count steps when I go up and I count
> them again on the way down. I count the
> number of cars passing by while waiting
> for my ride. I count the seconds between
> ocean waves and also between lightning
> and thunder claps. I count tiles in bath-
> rooms, usually for each color. And I even
> count pavement squares while walking
> city sidewalks. It's this last one that net-
> ted me $56.82 in found money last year.
> And it was also my downfall last week.
> I was walking as I regularly do, head
> down, focused on my count, comparing
> it to the previous day's numbers, when...*

Finish the story.

147

Write a story composed of a series of tweets back and forth between two people. Tweets are a maximum 140 characters—including punctuation.

Start with: "I miss you already..."

148

Start a story like this:

> *She checked her coat pockets, her pants pockets, and her purse—twice. Then she panicked.*

Finish the story.

For this exercise, you will write four different opening paragraphs for four different stories. Each of the four stories will begin with two people putting fresh linens on a bed. What will change is who these people are.

Here are the four pairs of people, one for each opening paragraph:

       1 — A nurse and a hospice worker

       2 — A mother and a father

       3 — Newlyweds

       4 — A parent and a college student

150

Write part of a tell-all article for a women's magazine where you interview someone famous. Include at least a dozen of your questions with (made-up) answers from the famous person.

151

Compose a story about a family that lost almost everything when the stock market crashed. Start the story one year after the crash. Make sure to include the following:

      How are they faring?

      Where do they live?

      What changed over the year?

      What lessons were learned?

Time to try your hand at writing a fable about a ferret and a rabbit.

The moral at the end of the story is: Be accountable and take responsibility.

U sing a maximum of fifteen lines on the page, write a very short and complete romance story that ends tragically.

Start with: "Her breast heaved with…"

Write a story about someone who is both house-sitting and pet-sitting.

Use foreshadowing at the start of your story to forewarn and prepare the reader for a heartrending ending.

155

Try starting and ending a story with the same four words. For instance: "I checked my watch..." and "...I checked my watch."

156

Write a third-person narrative story about two people whose names are never mentioned. Use only the pronouns "he," "she," "him," and "her." Have it take place in a cemetery and include a bit of dialogue as well.

B egin a gothic novel. Set it in a huge country home in the eighteenth century and include both a menacing ghost as well as a strained love relationship. Write until you reach a good breaking point.

Start with: "The doorbell to Malmure Manor sounded..."

Start with:

> *You have a thriving business called Type*
> *A. In the local directory, it is merely listed*
> *as an import company. But to everyone*
> *in the after-dark crowd, you are known*
> *simply as Bloodman. You provide acces-*
> *sories, accoutrements, clothing, sleeping*
> *quarters, and all sorts of services to vam-*
> *pires. Of course, you have to keep really*
> *odd hours, but the loyal clientele certainly*
> *makes up for it. One evening, as everyone*
> *was emerging from their coffins...*

Finish the story.

Compose an essay on the advantages of being a couch potato. Support your underdog theory with at least three real-life anecdotes. Include references to contrasting points of view. And tie the whole piece together with a strong finish that will sway at least a few people to your way of life.

Write a story that uses these sensory combinations: the sound of cotton balls, the taste of a magnifying glass, the feel of loud music.

Start with: "None of us ever expected to..."

Create a story about a character who collects soda cans and other metals from trash bins. Here are some questions to consider when writing:

> What got him or her started?
>
> Does he or she do it out of necessity, charity, or for some other reason?
>
> Does he or she do it by day or by night?
>
> Does he or she do it alone?
>
> What does he or she wear while doing it?
>
> What does he or she use to collect the metal in?
>
> Does doing this help or hurt his or her pride?

Write your own writing prompt! Simply fill in all the blanks below:

> Write a [choose a genre] story that takes place at [location] during [specific time period].
>
> A(n) [item] will be vital to the plot.
>
> Your main character's motivation is [emotion].
>
> Include this word in your story: [verb ending with "ing"] as well as this word: [adverb ending with "ly"].
>
> For a starting phrase, use something you would read in a fortune cookie.

While you're in a creative frame of mind, go ahead and use your prompt to write the story.

If you enjoyed doing this, you can use the same formula to create many more prompts.

Write a story that includes each of the following five words—twice. Each has more than one definition, so please use a different meaning each time.

      1 — crane

      2 — leaves

      3 — shake

      4 — mold

      5 — company

Start with: "We had a ball…"

Start with:

> *Maybe riding the subway in a Halloween costume wasn't the greatest idea. But there I was, dressed as a Caesar salad, grasping the overhead ring with one hand, holding my oversized salad tongs in the other. I don't have the greatest balance, and I especially don't like bumping into people, so normally I sit down when I ride into the city. But with all the leafy greens dangling off my shirt and a big cardboard bowl around my butt, it just wasn't a possibility. When the train jolted, I...*

Continue the story.

Pick a character from this list:

> Princess, CEO, Homeless person,
> Bank teller, Teenage girl, Tennis pro,
> Guru, Archaeologist. Postal worker,
> Model

Pick a motivation from the following list:

> Anger, Revenge, Love, Reputation,
> Hunger, Fear, Fame, Religious belief,
> Peer pressure, Greed

A body of water will play a crucial role in this story about your chosen character who has this motivation.

Does your character succeed or fail in terms of the motivation?

Write a platonic love story where the object of affection is an animal.

Start with: "The minute our eyes met..."

Fill fifteen lines with pure description about one of the ten listed locations. Return again to try your hand at the other nine.

> 1 — A path in the woods
>
> 2 — A horse show
>
> 3 — An arboretum
>
> 4 — A car race
>
> 5 — A baseball game
>
> 6 — A carnival
>
> 7 — A ski slope
>
> 8 — Picnic grounds
>
> 9 — A lake
>
> 10 — A beach

Start each of your pieces with this phrase: "At first glance..."

Describe a walk down Main Street in a town from your imagination. Draw a map if it helps.

Who do you see? Who stops to talk? Where do you step inside? Where do you linger? What's new since the last time you were there? What do you miss? What do you wish for this place?

Write a list titled "Ten People I Don't Ever Want to Meet."

Pick one of them and write about what happens when you do (hypothetically) meet.

170

Where we grow up often has a big impact on who we grow up to be. Write a list of adjectives or short descriptive phrases that describe your hometown or your childhood neighborhood. When you are done, go back through the list and underline all the words/phrases that also describe you.

Use these phrases in a short memoir or autobiographical writing.

171

Start with:

> *I can't believe he didn't text. He said he would. Well, Anna said that he said that he would. Who does he think he is? He should know better than to try and avoid me. I've done it before and I will do it again. I will stand in front of his house and throw my old stuffed animals—or maybe something bigger this time—at his window until he acknowledges me. We have to talk at some point. I mean, really talk. But texting is a good start. It's better than nothing. I just checked my phone. Only Anna. Looking to see if he texted. Doesn't she know I will text her the second he does? I always do. Now she's making me mad, too.*

To complete this story, you'll need to add four more paragraphs.

Here is the setup for a story being told in the first person:

At a meeting in the mayor's office, you just found out that the area's biggest benefactor donated 200 snails to the town. These aren't your average pet snails or even snails to be eaten; rather, they are almost-human-sized, unpainted snail sculptures. They are to be used as part of a big community art project and then auctioned off. For the last two years, as public relations director, your main job has been to attract new industry to the area by dispelling your town's reputation as a backward, slow place. In no way, shape, or form do you want snails to be linked to your town!

How do you solve the problem and keep everyone happy and still convince tourists and industry you are not slow as snails?

173

Using a blanket or quilt, go through your life, year by year, and recall episodes and memories that are triggered by these items. When you find a juicy one, run with it and write the story.

Create a piece about a thirty-year-old whose life is going well until she or he encounters an obstacle.

Choose from one of the four obstacles below. Remember to come back and try your hand at the other three.

  1 — In the wrong place at the wrong time

  2 — A health issue

  3 — An ugly breakup

  4 — A job loss

Start with: "In the best of times..."

175

Write one scene from a story where a life-or-death situation emerges. Start in the middle of the story and focus on this scene with the arising situation. Flesh it out and make it as realistic as possible. Scare yourself if you have to.

Think back to a time when you reacted out of character to a situation. Maybe you said yes to doing something that typically scares you. Or maybe you were outright aggressive when you are normally timid. Or perhaps you quivered in a corner when you would have expected yourself to be brave.

Write about it in detail, capturing the surprise you felt so your reader can also feel it.

177

Pick two very different characters you know well from two different books, comics, movies, or TV shows. Lock them in a room with only two chairs, one table, a refrigerator filled with snacks and beverages, and a bathroom off to the side. They have to stay there for twenty-four hours straight.

Write about what happens. Make it ugly at some point. Use lots of dialogue.

Create a suspense story about a ranch hand, a promise, and a traveler. Draw your writing out, like the way your ranch hand speaks. Fill at least two pages with your prose.

Start with:

> The news media is saying it's a stunt because I build tree houses for the rich and famous. They don't know anything. They're referring to me as Tree House Charlie. My name is Chaz, for Christsake. C-H-A-Z, which doesn't rhyme with the word "tree." Until my kid got sick, I never did anything to call attention to myself, my business, or my family. I just did my work, hung out on my boat, fished, and was as good a dad and husband as I knew how to be. But that hospital is guilty of malpractice and I want the world to know. Instead, calls are coming in to build more tree houses for rich jerks. Why doesn't anyone get it? What else do I have to do to make my point?

Finish the story.

180

In approximately 100 words, write a children's story about a boat, a boy, and a one-dollar bill. Make it very visual so that it would be easy to illustrate.

181

Create a short story with a big dose of mystery about a woman where a ukulele plays a pivotal role. Make a note to keep it short, to the point, and no more than 250 words.

182

This piece will be written from the point of view of a smartphone that has magical powers. Perhaps it can read minds, shrink whoever touches it, fly around taking aerial shots of embarrassing moments, or something else of your invention. Have the phone tell what it does to keep from being purchased because it is having too much fun pulling pranks in the store.

Write a funny science-fiction story about a robot, a croissant, and a sword. Make it 300 words maximum.

You have been hired to write a thirty-second late-night TV commercial for a new product—smart underwear. Write the text for the commercial along with stage directions. Include props and some preshot video summaries. The spokesperson has a strong Boston accent, which you might want to take into consideration. Have fun with it.

Robert Cormier made a great point when he said, "The beautiful part of writing is that you don't have to get it right the first time, unlike, say, a brain surgeon." Here's a chance to enjoy the luxury of working on a piece until you get it right.

Grab what you wrote for another exercise in this book or retrieve some other short piece of your writing. Read it out loud, listening for things that don't sound right. Relying only on your ear, make changes. Keep reading the piece out loud and making changes until you like what you hear.

186

Your protagonist owns a private investigation agency whose motto is "We Solve It—Or It's Free." Start the story with:

> *I love the moment in a case where I know I got the goods. I can actually feel the payment jangle in my pocket. And, I equally hate the moment where I show proof of said goods to my clients, because most of them scream, "You're a liar! You made that up just to get paid!" as the door slams behind them. Most come back with their tail between their legs, often within a few minutes. My last case, however, was a bit different...*

Finish the story.

Write a story where the plot is about two characters whose families have a long history of rivalry. The arrival of an old neighbor sparks things up again.

Choose one of these four settings as the backdrop for your story. Remember to come back and give the other three a try, too:

1 — Dentist's office

2 — Car manufacturing plant

3 — Funeral

4 — TV station

188

Write a story about a man who finds a diamond ring and the trials and tribulations that occur as he attempts to find its rightful owner. Have him discover that not everyone is as honest as he is.

Pick two characters from below and write a conversation that takes place between them where one is giving advice to the other. Come back another time and pick different combinations. In each conversation, there must be some emphasis on a glass or glasses.

Here are your character choices:

Nun

Chiropractor

Chemist

Dog groomer

Comic

Exterminator

Mafia godfather

Insurance adjustor

Taxidermist

Latin teacher

Drummer

Pastor

190

Using the three criteria below, one per paragraph, write a complete story in three paragraphs:

1 — In the introductory paragraph, write about a character who is so busy being jealous, her life almost completely passes her by.

2 — In the middle paragraph, create an episode or event that causes her to take stock.

3 — In the third paragraph of conclusion, describe her life after this event.

Does she change? Does she stay the same?

Sometimes the grooms come to my chapel dressed as Elvis. And once in a while I'll get a lady in drag. But for the most part, they're in tuxes and gowns and I'm the only one in costume. After delivering their nuptials, I serenade every couple with my best, heartfelt rendition of "Can't Help Falling in Love with You" a la early Elvis. One Valentine's Day, after my fiftieth ceremony, and ten more left to go, my voice ran out. I sent my assistant to the Strip to find an impersonator to impersonate me impersonating Elvis... and one who could wing the part of minister without ratting me out. She came back with...

What happens next?

Use this personal ad to spark a story idea:

> "R. — Know u saw me in the mkt bc u
> turned red b4 u put ur head down. Let's
> work it out abt H. & the B. Pls meet.
> Cereal aisle, Thurs 6.—J."

193

Start with:

> *That was the moment where everything changed...*

Finish the story.

194

Write a story that includes these three made-up words: "DAPI," "INOPHE," "IAR." They can be anything you like—names, places, adjectives, verbs. Let your instincts choose, and let your reader deduce the meaning through context.

Start with this phrase: "After the ceremonial candle was lit..."

Holiday and birthday presents are fun to receive. Sometimes, when we're not supposed to, we find them in advance. Write about either searching for a present or happening upon one that was supposed to be a surprise.

Start with: "In the…"

Your story is going to be about a motorcycle. It takes place in the present day but also includes a few flashbacks. Keep your flashbacks brief, vivid, and in narrative form. Return to your regular story as quickly as possible after you make your point, give your story some necessary history, or provide your character with some depth.

Start with: "The sound of the..."

Finish this story:

> *Out of breath, I raced up the steps, barely on time for my appointment. But hanging on the closed door of the headquarters of the Intergalactic Nanospecific Telegrammatic Operative (INTO) was a sign that read...*

198

Write a tale that follows one of these three tried-and-true formulas. Add your own personal touch so that your story rises above being a complete cliché. Come back and try out the other two in the future.

> 1 — A character commits a perfect crime but forgets one little thing.

> 2 — A character carries out a revenge plot but on the wrong person.

> 3 — Boy meets girl, boy loses girl, boy gets girl.

Pen a story where your character's fear escalates. In the beginning, it's nothing more than benign worry. But as the tale progresses, it becomes full-fledged terror. Of course, it's up to you whether or not there's a happy ending.

Choose one of the five fears provided and remember to come back and try your hand at the other four.

1 — Monsters

2 — Heights

3 — Ghosts

4 — Death

5 — Flying

Look up some nursery rhymes and pick one to parody (spoof). The easiest way to start is to choose a topic that is entertaining yet far from the original. Subjects of universal appeal like buying shoes or eating pizza or pet ownership are best. Then brainstorm words that fit the rhyme scheme, and slowly but surely a funny parody will grow.

201

Write a science fiction story that takes place on Earth in the year 2525. Your main character, Bot Ro, lives on a flying boat near what used to be Dallas, Texas. Include political satire—in the form of poking fun at today's politics via this new place and time—in your tale.

According to children's book author and essayist E.B. White, "Don't write about Man, write about a man."

With that in mind, start with: "He held his..."

Take a moment and look at your cell phone. If you don't have one, look at your home phone. Think about a particularly emotional conversation you had on this phone. Tell the story here.

Start with either of these: "When I dialed..." or "When I picked up..."

In Landonose, nothing smells as it should; rather, everything smells like something with which it rhymes. Trees smell like peas, roads smell like toads, money smells like honey, and bells smell like shells. Frequent sniffing, whiffing, and smelling are all considered acts of politeness.

Have your story take place in Landonose, starting with this: "From the time I was little, I knew that returning smells to normal was…"

Look straight ahead and imagine that everything in sight looks like it was in a black and white picture. If it helps, frame the view with your hands to make it the shape of a photograph. Write about the moment (perhaps long ago) that prompted the photographer to take this picture. Also write about what happened to the photo such that it has ended up in your possession.

Add twenty years to your age. You are still you, just twenty years from now. Write as this more mature person.

Start with: "Looking back at all the cakes and candles..."

207

Write a breakup letter to your credit card. Tell it off. Don't mince words or go easy on it.

S tarting lines come in all lengths. Choose one of these eight that appeals to you and write until you fill a whole page. Remember to return to this page seven more times and try the others, too.

1 — Clouds...

2 — Until now...

3 — The dimmed lights...

4 — While waiting for the...

5 — The fortune in the cookie...

6 — We all danced to their song...

7 — The shock of the loud alarm catapulted...

8 — Almost always misunderstood, he once and for all...

Write a 150-word story about winning some-thing. Your mission is to convey a feeling of contagious excitement. Let the words bubble from you. Keep your sentences short and sometimes just use phrases to show your emotion. Your style and word selection should show the mood as much as the actual content of the story does.

Surfers truly have their own language. Here are some phrases that, when inserted properly, will make you sound like you know what you are talking about when you write about surfing.

Amped—excited
Anglin'—turning left or right on a wave
Ankle busters—small waves
Baggies—loose, boxer-type swim trunks
Back down—decide not to take off on a wave
Banzai—a gung-ho yell
Curl—portion of the wave that is breaking
Meatball—yellow flag with a black circle indicating
  "No Surfing"
Nailed—get badly wiped out
Pounder—hard-breaking wave
Walking the nose—moving forward on the board
  toward the front

Try to use as many of these as possible in a piece that begins: "I took one look at the Hodad—the pale kid who started hanging around the beach about a week ago—and instinctively knew that even though he wanted to be one of our new gremlins, he wasn't cut out for it. But no one could stop him, not even me. To him, surfing was…"

211

Think about a moment in your life when you were intimidated. Describe where you were, what was happening, who was with you, why you were there, and how you felt—physically and emotionally—before, during, and after the moment.

Write a story that takes place in a small-town diner at a table where six of the local men gather every morning for breakfast. This morning is different because a news van just pulled up out front.

Start with: "Hey, Vic, see her? That's that one from Channel 6..."

213

Compile a list of ten words associated with inclement weather.

Use all of them in a piece about a family reunion. Do not mention weather at all in your story.

Write a one-page story that concludes with this quote from Malcolm X:

It is only after slavery and prison that the sweetest appreciation of freedom can come.

215

Write a ten-line prose poem in which you include the idiom "into thin air," as well as these five words: "swish," "cranberry," "lilacs," "sandpaper," "salty."

Time to build your descriptive muscle with some images of physical traits. You can use your own body viewed in a mirror, or subtly position yourself so you have an unobstructed view of another person. Write one paragraph of pure description for each of the five body parts provided. Experiment with metaphor and use unusual adjectives to paint a picture with words.

1 — Neck

2 — Ears

3 — Shoulders

4 — Nose

5 — Forehead

217

Finish this story:

> *All I had to do was watch her hands and I knew she was...*

Fill in the blank in the opening line and then finish the story.

> *I am not sure how or when I am going to drop this bomb—figuratively, of course—on _____[name of a person or people], but my window of time is quickly running out.*

219

Write a story titled "In The Fast Lane" in which your sentences are quick and the pacing is fast.

Start with: "My muscles..."

Start with:

> *My ex is a coward and a control freak who couldn't find a tiny wormhole in his big ego to let me mourn my mother-in-law's death in peace. As soon as I arrived at the funeral parlor, he sent our son— a boy experiencing death for the first time—to tell me to move to the back row. The sadness in my son's eyes as he asked me was heartbreaking. I was livid. And I was hurt.*

Finish the story.

Write a list of ten things you wish you had done when you were a child. Your list will look something like these:

>   1 — When I was eight, I wish I had joined the Girl Scouts like everyone else.
>
>   2 — When I was twelve, I wish I had yelled back at A.

When done, remove some of the opening phrases, add some transitional words, and link them to create a prose poem.

What follows is the first paragraph of a book written by George and Weedon Grossmith titled *The Diary of a Nobody*.

> *My dear wife Carrie and I have just been a week in our new house, "The Laurels," Brickfield Terrace, Holloway—a nice six-roomed residence, not counting basement, with a front breakfast-parlour. We have a little front garden; and there is a flight of ten steps up to the front door, which, by-the-by, we keep locked with the chain up. Cummings, Gowing, and our other intimate friends always come to the little side entrance, which saves the servant the trouble of going up to the front door, thereby taking her from her work. We have a nice little back garden which runs down to the railway. We were rather afraid of the noise of the trains at first, but the landlord said we should not notice them after a bit, and took 2 pounds off the rent. He was certainly right; and beyond the cracking of the garden wall at the bottom, we have suffered no inconvenience.*

Continue the story by writing the next paragraph or two.

Continue the story by writing the next paragraph or two.

223

Write a travelogue from the point of view of being a tourist in your own hometown. Describe the sights and sounds that you, as a local, cherish. Briefly mention the destinations every visitor seeks out but only to (negatively) compare them to the better ones you feature. Capture the excitement so that readers will want to enjoy them, too.

224

Using a marketplace as your primary location, write a story about a psychic who is assisting a retired police officer in solving an old cold case. The officer does not have permission to be investigating, but the case is too haunting to let go. Be inventive with your marketplace—flea market, shopping mall, fish market, flower market, bazaar, etc.

225

Write a story about a woman who, when she arches one eyebrow, communicates volumes. Make this method of nonverbal communication integral to your story by referencing it a few times. Also include a young man and a vase in your tale.

Start with: "It wasn't her..."

226

Write about a time when you were in flow and on top of your game. Describe what you were doing, where you were, and how you felt—physically and emotionally—during the time you were in the zone as well as right afterwards.

227

It's a rainy day, and it has triggered the memory of a similar day from your past. Write a letter to the friend or relative with whom you spent that day. Reminisce about it. Use anecdotes and lots of details.

It's time to review the footage on the nanny camera you hid in your son's playroom. You hope your suspicions aren't correct.

What do you see? And what do you do about it? Write the story.

Finish this press conference. Include questions from reporters and answers from witnesses, their attorney, the mayor, and the chief of police.

> Chief of police: *"I guess the people to best tell what occurred are the two witnesses. First is James Ernest Trollop, who goes by Trolley."*
>
> Trolley: *"Okay. Let me make a point. That night we were not high or drunk. We were cold, really cold. Um... uh... we are home-less. And, yes, we were sleeping—um, ille-gally—in the shed behind the elementary school. Both Ninny and I saw exactly the same thing."*

230

Finish this story:

"Hey, buddy. I think your luck just ran out."

231

Write a story about a snow globe, a quarter, and a Native American.

Start with: "I had never seen..."

Compose a story about a person on a quest. Over the course of the story, have him or her visit three different destinations. At the end of the story, he or she is substantially different from the onset.

Use dialogue to illustrate what transpires at each of the three destinations.

Write a dynamic, plot-busting chase scene that partially takes place in a wax museum.

Who is doing the chasing? Who is being chased? Why? What happens to the person being chased? What happens to the person doing the chasing? Is his or her heart really in it? What role did the museum play?

234

Start with:

> *As the sand and shallow water slipped under my feet and out to sea with the tide, something nicked my big toe. "God, I hate jellyfish!" I mumbled as I reached down. From under my toe I pulled out something round and metal. A gold coin—shiny, with uneven edges and all sorts of interesting markings. I palmed it and started to run back to our beach blanket. I don't know what made me stop mid-step, but I am sure glad it did. There, a mere two inches from my other big toe...*

Finish the story.

This tongue-in-cheek story is about a human-size parrot that is also a pirate. He wears an eye patch and is a great swashbuckler. He even has a pet human (the size of a parrot, of course) who sits on his shoulder at all times.

Tell the story of one of their adventures where, thanks to the human pet's intelligence, they were able to outsmart their adversaries and score some serious booty.

236

Write a story that takes place on a farm and is narrated by a child or a tween who was sent there from the city for a summer. As the story progresses and farm life becomes easier, let the narrator's vocabulary and speech reflect some of his or her internal changes as well. Perhaps he or she will sound less harsh or will start to use some local-color references and phrases.

Tell the true story of the most embarrassing or mortifying moment in your life. To make the telling easier, use a third-person narrator. Keep the entire tale to four paragraphs.

238

Write one totally true sentence about something you recall from second grade.

Use this sentence as a starter and completely fabricate a tale as told by someone else. It doesn't even have to be about second grade or school. Don't try to conjure your own memories. Instead, let your imagination run with the starter and see where you end up.

Go back and read what you wrote. Does it still sound like you? Or does it sound like someone else?

239

Write a story that takes place in a hotel and focuses on a cake, a bullfight, and a message.

A hotel clerk is your narrator. He or she relates the story but never gives his or her point of view or opinion. Rather, the clerk only repeats or passes along tidbits and opinions of others as well as things he or she has overheard from eavesdropping.

240

Compose a piece about an umbrella. Anything goes here—sharing one, losing one, one blowing inside out, never having one when you need one, owning a pink one as a kid, kissing under one—just run with the topic. Do this in six minutes. Let your thoughts rain onto the page. But when the time is up, you must stop and put away the umbrella for another rainy day.

Write a story about someone who hears voices. This could be somebody with mental problems, a novelist in the zone, a prophetic person, or someone on whom a prank is being played. You choose.

Start with: "Ignoring the voices is no longer a possibility."

242

Write about a ritual. It might be religious, superstitious, or something you do every week or once a year. When you describe it, use your voice like the lens of a camera where you capture the visuals of the ritual in words so the reader can see what you are doing.

243

Write about a time when you were performing or speaking on stage or in front of many people. First tell the story from your point of view in the present as if you are there now. Tell how you feel, how you think you look, and how well you are doing.

Then write about the same episode, also in the present, but from the point of view of someone who is in the audience—preferably someone who came specifically to see you. Write what they see, how you look to them, what it feels like to watch you, how they think you are faring and feeling.

Were there any words that you used in both pieces? Or were they 100 percent different?

244

Imagine that you are a hypochondriac. For about the last four hours, you've had a lower backache that has been getting progressively worse. Your therapist suggested you write through these episodes. So you pull out the brand new journal you bought last week and crack it open. Write your first entry.

When you are done writing, does your back feel better, worse, or the same? What do you do now?

245

Write a story that includes these three made-up words: "TREGE," "GNEPINU," "DICLANAR." They can be anything you like—names, places, adjectives, verbs. Let your instincts choose, and let your reader deduce the meaning through context.

Start with this phrase: "The group of birdwatchers..."

Start with this:

> *Crisp linens on a table that is set with fine china, sparkling silver, and glistening crystal. Light from the candelabra dances on the walls. A concerto plays quietly in the background. Suddenly, a deafening sound interrupts the perfect mood...*

Write about what happens next.

247

Think of setting up a brand new computer. Jot down some of the smells, textures, and emotions that come to mind. Use all the phrases and words you wrote down in a story that has absolutely nothing to do with computers.

Start your story with this: "The restaurateur took great pride in..."

Start with:

> *After three weeks of training, I was finally ready to give my first solo tour of the zoo. I was happy to see that my group was a fairly well-behaved bunch of students visiting from Russia. All went well in the reptile house, and the penguins were a big hit. However, when we entered the primate area...*

Finish the story.

If you are ever in need of a quick writing exercise, simply start with the word "he," add a verb, then fill a page. Here are twenty-six, one for each letter of the alphabet, to get you started:

> He acted, He burped, He chose,
> He drove, He exhaled, He flew,
> He groaned, He handed, He itched,
> He joshed, He kidded, He lisped,
> He mastered, He noted, He opted,
> He panned, He quizzed, He rang,
> He shouted, He trembled,
> He unopened, He verified,
> He wrestled, He X'd, He yo-yo'd,
> He zeroed.

Pick one now and fill an entire page. I invite you to come back and use the other twenty-five.

250

Start with:

> *Our usual crowd, complete with our slightly quirky rituals, was assembled around the table. There was Joe, constantly and mindlessly opening and closing his tin of spearmint lozenges with his right hand; Marley with her holey, faded pink knit shawl bunched up on her lap and her* Marley and Me *coffee mug filled to the brim with nothing but steaming hot water; and Bob B., wearing two pairs of glasses at the same time and sporting a third backup pair around his neck. When everyone was settled, I pulled out the...*

Finish the story.

251

Write a story that includes these three items:

      1 — A lecture

      2 — A tea kettle

      3 — A pair of dice

Start the story with this phrase: "It seemed like magic when..."

252

You are the space bar of a computer keyboard.
Write from this key's point of view.

Start with: "I cringe whenever he..."

253

A nne Lamott once said, "You just sit down and write every day for three or four hours. You do it like piano scales until you have a story to tell."

Based on your own successes and experiences, write a motivational essay with your advice to new writers or writers who are experiencing a lull in their writing practice.

Remember to practice what you preach!

254

Either select a character from a piece you have written or choose a character from a movie or book you love. This character spots a package in the middle of the road. At the moment, there is a lot of traffic and your character is not alone. What will your character do?

255

Cradling the award in your arms, you step up to the microphone.

What do you say?

Who do you thank?

How do you feel?

What is the award for?

Think back to a time when you were learning how to do something new—ride a bicycle, do yoga, play guitar, learn a new language.

Write about how you felt when you were trying to catch on.

Then fast forward to when you had your first "aha" moment in the process. Write about that, too.

You are Miss Etiquette for a local weekly news-
paper. You have a column due tomorrow, but
no one has written in for advice. To be honest, no
one has ever really written in. For the last four years
you have faked the entire column by getting your
friends, acquaintances, neighbors, and relatives to
give you questions. You are totally tapped out of
resources, so you decide to write to yourself about
your own dilemma. Start with:

> *Dear Miss Etiquette, I have not been hon-
> est at work. Every week I lie...*

You have been contracted to write a book-for-hire titled *Romance for the Partner Who Wears the Pants*.

Start by writing the introduction.

Start with:

> *In spite of the fact that he practically exploded into the room with his exaggerated swagger, his smile was surprisingly endearing. His muscles, rippling under his T-shirt, were indeed an added bonus. He headed directly toward...*

Finish the story.

260

The film *Magnum Force* ends with this line:

A man's got to know his limitations.

Use it as the first sentence in a new story that is not at all related to the theme or plot of that movie.

261

Here are five traits to help you create a character:

    1 — intuitive

    2 — only child

    3 — long, straight hair

    4 — flighty

    5 — gregarious

Continue adding traits until you can see a person emerge. Once you have a visual, write from this character's point of view.

Start with: "As soon as I opened the..."

262

Here is the who (a princess), what (a wish), when (year 2044), and where (the planet, PastaMosta) of a story.

It's up to you to supply the why as you write, starting with: "I desperately wanted to travel back in time to…"

263

Most stories about strangers seem to involve suspicion or danger. This is a shame because just about everyone has had some positive encounters with strangers.

Write about an experience you had with a particularly kind stranger.

You are on the phone with an animal psychic who is communicating with your recently deceased pet. She just explained to you that you will be able to hear her as she repeats your questions out loud, but she will also be sending images to your pet that you will not be able to see. When your pet "talks back" to her via images, she will translate them into words for you. Play out the conversation between the pet psychic, your deceased pet, and you.

Start with:

> *Hi,* [insert pet name and all pet nick-names here]. *My name is Isabella and I am here with* [insert the name you use when talking to your pet to refer to yourself]. *I am sending you an image of me. When you get it, please send back an image of you and where you are.*

Take it from here.

Insects are often overlooked when it comes to writing. The good news for you is that overlooked matter can provide some of the best fodder for writing. Think back through insect stories of your life—watching ants, being stung by a bee, running from a spider, hearing about Lyme disease, catching a lightning bug—and pick one.

Write about it, starting with: "Sometimes it's the little things..."

266

We all have stories of weddings, funerals, and other big life events that take place in churches, synagogues, and mosques. Think of a time when you were in a house of worship that had nothing to do with religion and nothing to do with a rite-of-passage moment. Write about it.

Start with: "We weren't supposed to…"

267

There's nothing quite like having a good friend. But even good friends have their bad moments. Write about a time when you were a bad friend to someone. Confess on paper. Tell the story. Let it all hang out.

Think about an outstanding—good or bad—holiday meal spent with family or friends. Write about it from your point of view.

Then pick another person who was there and write about it again, but from their point of view.

Both times start with: "There were at least…"

Here are six traits of not one, but two characters:

      1 — persistent

      2 — emotional

      3 — worried

      4 — passionate

      5 — chunky

      6 — cocoa-skinned

Write a story of conflict about a heroin/heroine and a villain (good guy/bad guy) where both characters embody all of these traits.

Start with: "Similarities aside..."

You received the following email:

> *Dearest Madam, I saw your picture on Facebook and your smile provided me with much happiness. I am sorry if my son who is typing this has bad English because he learned it in YouTube videos. In your profile it says you are widow and philanthropist. The page translated these words for me. I am glad you no longer have sadness about your husband. Philanthropist provides me with much happiness because my little country, Dikar, requires financial assistance. My brother is King but he is not filled with happiness. He wanted to make our people happy so he spent all our money in search of rubies in very many wrong places. Now there are no finances left. In exchange for your philanthropist, we would like you to become our Queen and live in the palace. I am happy to hear back from you as soon as possible.*
>
> *Signed,*
>
> *Radik Kidar, Brother of the King of Dikar*

Time to write an answer.

In your mind, recall the home of a childhood friend. Write a walking tour through the home, describing the street, the lawn, the door, the play area, your friend's bedroom, etc. There were probably many textures, smells, and sounds in this home; try to include them.

After your written tour, go back to a spot in the home where you recall having a fun time. Write that story now.

Start with: "We were not…"

There are lots of writing prompts that have you write with your nondominant hand. This is one of those, but we're going to crank it up a notch or two. You will write with your nondominant hand, but you will also turn the page forty-five degrees. This means you will be writing with the paper in landscape orientation rather than portrait. And to make it even more challenging, you will not look at the page; rather, you will stare straight ahead while writing.

Start with: "We had a staring contest..."

When you are done, use the same starter again, but switch the pen to your regular hand and rotate the page to its usual orientation. Still stare straight ahead while you write.

273

Write a list titled "Ten Things I Don't Ever Want to Do on Summer Vacation."

Pick one of them and write about it as if you did do it. Fill an entire page.

Start with: "That summer wasn't..."

274

Alma Zima and Bart Yarrow were just married. They sat next to each other in first grade, where they secretly shared a kiss. Alma's family moved away at the end of that school year. They never saw each other again until one year ago, when they were surprisingly reunited while standing in line at Disney World.

Tell the story of their romance and nuptials in the form of a wedding write-up for a local print or on-line newspaper.

There are certain items in our lives that we often take for granted. The keys on our key ring, for example. It's time to give these keys the love they deserve. Write a mushy, demonstrative love letter to your keys. Tell them why you love them. Tell them how you plan to treat them in the future. Romance them.

Monsta, your family dog, has figured out a way to break through the invisible fence. When he leaves, he stays away for a few days at a stretch. Even after you have repaired the fence once and then replaced it, it has happened three months in a row. To figure out how he does it, you put a pet camera on him. Three weeks have gone by and he has been a good boy. The very day when you were starting to feel silly for putting the camera on him and were contemplating its removal, Monsta took off for parts unknown.

Write from the point of view of Monsta. Describe why you waited so long, how you escape, where you go, what you do, who you meet, and what prompts you to return home.

Just let the video run and the story will unfold. Start with: "It was a kind of yucky day and I..."

277

Your story begins:

> *We were at a party when I told my friends I was thinking about dropping out of college and heading to LA to become a screenwriter. No one took me seriously. I still don't know why at that very moment I felt compelled to blurt it out. But once those words made their way through my lips, turning what had been a fantasy into the reality of sound, something inside me shifted. It took me another year, but here I am.*

Take it from here.

There was a partial building collapse and three people happened to be driving by at the moment it occurred—you and two other strangers. The three of you rushed to the scene and helped everyone inside escape. You instructed them to flee for fear of a total collapse and also to call for help (this was before the time of cell phones). On your last trip in, the building collapsed even more, and now the three of you are trapped in the cellar of the building.

Here are the three people, none of whom are locals:

> 1 — An ex-con driving through the area in a stolen vehicle
>
> 2 — A traveling salesperson who was fired yesterday and is heading home three states away
>
> 3 — A printing press repair expert in transit from an airport to a city another hour away

Assign one role to yourself.

Once you all come to after the collapse, you realize you don't hear any noises from outside. That may be because the collapse is still echoing in your ears.

What do the three of you do now? Write the story.

Here is the first paragraph of the novel *Pere Goriot*, written by Honoré de Balzac. Translated into English, the title is *Father Goriot*:

> *Mme. Vauquer (nee de Conflans) is an elderly person, who for the past forty years has kept a lodging-house in the Rue Nueve-Sainte-Genevieve, in the district that lies between the Latin Quarter and the Faubourg Saint-Marcel. Her house (known in the neighborhood as the Maison Vauquer) receives men and women, old and young, and no word has ever been breathed against her respectable establishment; but, at the same time, it must be said that as a matter of fact no young woman has been under her roof for thirty years, and that if a young man stays there for any length of time it is a sure sign that his allowance must be of the slenderest. In 1819, however, the time when this drama opens, there was an almost penniless young girl among Mme. Vauquer's boarders.*

Continue the tale by writing the next paragraph or two.

In pencil, draw a medium-size outline of a shape like a star, heart, football, ball, arrow, pencil, or cube. Now write, starting at the top of the page. Do your best to make sure your story makes reference to the shape in some way. When you get to the outline of the shape, write all around it, but never inside it. Write until you get to the bottom of the page. Then go back and erase your pencil-drawn shape. When you hold up the page and look at it from afar, the shape will really stand out. When you get close, you will be able to read the words.

If you need a starter, use this: "She yelled, 'You best start to shape up real soon, or...'"

Here are six occupations and six physical traits. Pair up a name and a trait and then write from this person's point of view. Use other pairings for future writings.

1 — Stay-at-home parent

2 — Attorney

3 — Stand-up comic

4 — Chef

5 — Graphic designer

6 — Surgeon

1 — Has a glass eye

2 — Limps

3 — Spits when talks

4 — Has a lisp

5 — Is missing a middle finger

6 — Has tics

Start with: "Not much was at stake..."

282

Start with:

> *There is a window in my room. I like to look at it. Tonight I see all dark. And, too, I see my face that is sad. I am try not to cry, but I want to go back my country. I do not want to live with Mister Kevin. I want...*

Finish the story.

283

Your job is to write an acceptance speech for your boss, a candidate who just won an election. Your boss is sure she or he can make good on all the promises that were made during the campaign— except one. And, lucky you, your boss feels like now is the best time to mention the one exception.

You think you have figured out an excellent reason why *not* meeting this one promise will still be beneficial to and please the majority of your boss's constituency. But can you communicate it in the allotted four minutes before the onslaught of the confetti and balloons?

Give it a try.

284

Fill in the blanks in the sentence and then finish the story.

My first love was _____ [name or thing/ item] when I was _____ [age]. I knew it was love because...

Think back over the last week or so. Write down three things you recall that made you smile. Then write three things that annoyed you.

Look over all six items and pick one to use in a piece that begins: "It wasn't a big thing, but…"

Your local paper has a phone line reserved for residents and visitors to call in and rant about, share opinions on, or offer praise regarding people, places, and things in your town. There is a three-minute cutoff for the line's voice message system. Instead of calling in, here's your chance to voice off—in writing—about something in your community. To be fair, set a timer for three minutes so you don't exceed the limit.

287

You are two hours late to a dinner party hosted by a new friend you are dating. List twenty excuses that might just work and get you off the hook. Review the list and pick one and run with it. Elaborate and embellish with colorful details that make it such a good story, anyone would want to forgive you for being late.

Fill in these sentences based on a character named Olaf Sigmundson:

At least ten times a week, he _____

Whenever he is unhappy, he _____

His favorite pastime is _____

He always needs to be reminded to _____

When his work week is done, he _____

He enjoys watching _____

He needs to start _____

Write about him starting with: "The bell..."

P eople you expect to meet only once—and in passing—are often the perfect audience. In this writing, you are on a train between two cities you are visiting as a tourist. Tell the passenger next to you about an event you have never shared with anyone else.

Start with: "Traveling helps me remember..."

I t's best to steer clear of politics and religion at parties and social get-togethers. But when it comes to writing, there are no rules or limitations.

Can you describe your feelings about politics in a dozen words or less? Give it a try.

Now write the memory of your first exposure to something political. Try to do it in one paragraph. If this leaves you wanting to write more, keep going.

If you feel you've covered it all, move on to the next topic.

Can you describe your feelings about religion in a dozen words or less? Give it a try.

Now write the memory of your first exposure to something religious. Try to do it in one paragraph. If you feel you want to write more, go for it.

291

Write a Sherlock Holmes story in which Watson solves the case.

292

Time to write three haiku on three different topics. As a refresher, a haiku is a three-line poem with a total of seventeen syllables—five syllables in the first line, seven in the middle, five in the last line.

Your three topics are:

> 1 — A sport
>
> 2 — A disease
>
> 3 — A job

For this exercise, you will need a book in one of your favorite genres—particularly a genre in which you would like to practice writing. Make sure it's a book with chapters.

Open it to a random page and let your finger drop down. On your paper, write the word on which your finger landed. If it's "the" or "a" or another short, common word, use the next word that is not. Do this a total of four times, opening the book to a different page each time, until you have four words on your page.

Now flip through the book until you come to the first page of a chapter. Copy the opening sentence of this chapter onto your page. Use this sentence as your starter and include all four words in your piece. Make sure you write in the same genre as the book.

Your audience directly influences your style and content. Take the topic of bullying and write about it four different ways—one for each of the audiences listed below.

1 — Middle-school students

2 — Police recruits

3 — Teachers

4 — Senior citizens

Finish the story using bird puns whenever and wherever you can.

My cousin is an Angry Bird. I tried out for the part, but they said my face wasn't round enough. I was pretty jealous of him, especially when all the girls flocked to his side. But when I found out that in the video game, he was going to be launched over and over again from a slingshot, I was relieved. I am not one for pain. The last time I flew into a window I had a bruised beak, a wounded wing, and an awful headache for a week. Ever since my cousin became famous, he's been impossible to be around. At first we thought it was a phase, so we indulged his flight of fancy. But today he really ruffled our feathers when...

296

Write a story where gloves play an important role.

Do not use these words: "hand(s)," "arm(s),"
"finger(s)," "warm," "cold," "mittens," "winter."

Start with: "The Lost and Found..."

Write a ten-question Q & A where a very famous writer is interviewing you about your literary accomplishments. Include at least ten questions and your answers.

Think big and speak inventively when you answer. Make stuff up!

Write an opinion piece—often called an op-ed—about why it should be mandatory to have art and music in schools.

Most opinion pieces are about 600 words long, use informal language, are persuasive, are extremely subjective (it's your perspective, after all), start with a summary sentence, have a few follow-up and supportive paragraphs, and end with how readers can take action.

Maybe you should submit it for publication.

299

Using a window as a starting point, go through your life, year by year, and recall episodes and memories that are triggered by all these different windows. When you find a juicy one, run with it and write the story.

300

See if you can draw this story to a close by adding only three more paragraphs:

> *When I heard that pop, my first thought was that my career was probably fin-ished. My second thought was how much doggone pain I was in. But I can be a real stubborn SOB, so I refused the ambulance. A guy's gotta have his pride, you know? I sat down on the bench and waved off any help. At first I really was A-OK. But about fifteen minutes later, I was pretty sure I was going to faint. As I was reaching out for something to steady myself, out of nowhere, this angel with brown wavy hair and a dimple on her right cheek appeared and held my arm. She said she was an EMT who was going to pose as my girlfriend to get me out of there. I leaned against her, and as I thought about love, I passed out.*

Write about an activity you really don't like—despise, perhaps. Do not mention what the activity is in the writing.

When you are done, read it to others and see if they can guess what you were describing. If they guess things other than your intended activity, go back and add more specifics that would rule out their guesses.

302

Write an internal monologue that takes place inside the mind of a clown while he or she is performing at a kiddie party.

Start with: "At least today's kids..."

303

Start your story with:

> *After it was critiqued for not having a plot, I sulked for about a month and then threw the manuscript into a box and tossed it into a closet. That was over ten years ago. But in the last few days, I have not been able to get the main character of that book out of my head. I can't believe after all these years, she has decided to take up residence in my heart and brain —again. I keep seeing everything through her eyes and hearing her voice in my ears. I don't know if I should laugh, cry, or run. I do know unearthing that manuscript would be akin to conducting an archaeological dig.*

To find out what the author does, finish the story in your own words.

Bonnie Neubauer is the author of motivational writing books including *The Write-Brain Workbook Revised & Expanded Edition—400 Exercises to Liberate Your Writing* and *Take Ten for Writers* (Writer's Digest Books). She is also the inventor of *Story Spinner*, a handheld and digital tool for generating millions of creative writing exercises.

When she's not dreaming up writing prompts or running fun and funny workshops, Bonnie can be found playing, teaching, or designing board games. With her love of words and language, it's no surprise her first published game, *ADJitation* (BreakingGames.com), contains sixty-four cubes with different adjectives on all sides.

Bonnie lives in suburban Philadelphia surrounded by way more than a few of her favorite things, which include books, games, an iPad, pet cats, friends, extended family, and a wonderful husband. Follow her on Twitter @NeuBon or check out her (rarely updated) website, www.BonnieNeubauer.com.